**Journey**Through®

James

30 Biblical Insights by **Douglas Estes**

Our Daily Bread Publishing™

Requests for permission to quote
from this book should be directed to:

Permissions Department
Our Daily Bread Publishing
PO Box 3566
Grand Rapids, MI 49501

Or contact us by email at
permissionsdept@odb.org

Design by Joshua Tan
Typeset by Grace Goh

ISBN 978-1-64070-078-9

Printed in the United States of America
21 22 23 24 25 26 27 28 / 8 7 6 5 4 3

Preface

Life is hard. You know this, and James, a pastor for years, knew this too.

Throughout history, the church has struggled with the book of James. It is not about the life of Christ or history of the church; it is not a prediction of what will happen; it is not high-minded theology. That is not why James was written. I hope you will see this immediately. The book of James is practical, and sometimes its practicality can seem small compared to the lofty issues raised throughout Christian history. James wrote his letter to give simple yet profound guidance to his readers on living in a way that properly points our attention to God.

At each juncture of your life, you will have to choose between a way that draws you closer to God and one that draws you closer to the world. You will have to choose between two kinds of wisdom. And you cannot be, as James will say, "of two minds" about the direction of your life.

Over the next thirty days, you will see how James weaves a number of different themes together in his letter as he returns repeatedly to topics such as wisdom, faith, trials, actions, speaking, and avoiding evil—practical concerns for people who need practical answers to live their lives to the fullest.

I pray that the next thirty days will challenge you to move closer to being a "single-minded person," one who has the mind of Christ and who pursues the kind of wisdom that lasts—the wisdom that comes from God.

May God bless you richly,

Douglas Estes

We're glad you've decided to join us on a journey into a deeper relationship with Jesus Christ!

For more than sixty years, we have been known for our daily devotional, *Our Daily Bread*. Many readers enjoy the engaging, inspiring, and relevant articles that point them to God and the wisdom and promises of His unchanging Word, the Bible.

Building on the foundation of *Our Daily Bread*, we have developed this Bible study series to help believers spend time with God in His Word, book by book. We trust that this daily meditation on the Bible will draw you into a closer relationship with Him through our Lord and Savior, Jesus Christ.

How to use this resource

READ: This book is designed to be read alongside God's Word as you journey with Him. It offers explanatory notes to help you understand the Scriptures in fresh ways.

REFLECT: The questions are designed to help you respond to God and the Bible, letting Him change you from the inside out.

RECORD: The space provided allows you to keep a diary of your journey as you record your thoughts and jot down your responses.

An Overview

The book of James is a book about wisdom. Providing guidance for its readers to help them to make wise decisions, it stands in a long tradition of Jewish writing that we call "wisdom literature." With His use of parables and pithy sayings, Jesus is part of the same tradition as well.

In the history of the church, the book of James has often played second fiddle to the theological powerhouses of Paul and John. James is shorter, and perhaps a bit more subtle and thoughtful. It is not as memorable for many Christians, because the very thing that it wants to convey—thoughtful wisdom development—occurs only when patiently applied to our lives. Nevertheless, James plays a vital role in rounding out the New Testament.

The writer of the letter is James, the brother of Jesus and pastor of the church of Jerusalem. James's place among the first generation of Christians was unique: he was not only the half-brother of Jesus but also a Jewish Christian descended from David; witness to the public ministry and resurrection of Jesus; pastor of the "mother church" of the early Christian movement in Jerusalem; and martyr for the cause of Christ.

Structure of James

Chapter 1	Trials, blessings, temptation, religion, and wisdom
Chapter 2	How faith integrates with action
Chapter 3	How speech and wise living determine the course of our lives
Chapter 4	A call to be obedient to God and to turn away from the world
Chapter 5	Dangers of greed and importance of patience and prayer

Key Verse

"If any of you lacks wisdom, you should ask God, who gives generously to all without finding fault, and it will be given to you." —James 1:5

Day 1

Read James 1:1–4

As James begins his letter, he gives his name but does not identify himself as a pastor in Jerusalem. Nor does he mention that he is the brother of Jesus. Instead, he is simply "a servant of God and of the Lord Jesus Christ" (James 1:1). James has submitted his will to that of God, as a slave to a master. And not just God, generally speaking, but the Lord Jesus, the Messiah.

James writes to "the twelve tribes" (v. 1). Was he also writing to Gentiles (like us today)? Yes, but indirectly. His primary concern was the Jewish Christians of Israel. Just as Paul often wrote to Gentiles without excluding Jews (Galatians 2:7), here James writes to Jews without excluding Gentiles.

James writes in the way Jesus taught, akin to how wise men in the centuries before taught. Instead of covering a topic and then moving on to the next, James weaves a few key ideas together in his letter. These ideas ebb and flow like the tide, coming and going as he leads his reader through important issues.

James begins with encouragement for dealing with trials whenever they arise: we should "consider it pure joy" when we face trials as followers of Jesus (James 1:2). That's not how we usually feel about them!

James does not elaborate on the kinds of trials his readers may face, but there are many different kinds that can test our faith (see Romans 5:3). The reason we should feel this way about trials is not that we like to suffer or want to prove anything. Instead, we should consider it a "joy" to go through trials because they have the effect of increasing our faith.

James explains that trials are a necessary part of growing to maturity because they produce endurance ("perseverance," James 1:3), and endurance must "finish its work" in us so that we may be mature and complete (v. 4). This endurance is our patient, faithful attitude in the midst of trials. To explain this completion through endurance, James uses descriptive words that depict both getting to the end and filling a full portion (v. 4). **These words point to the idea that as Christians face difficulties, they will remain faithful, and this faithfulness will bring them to spiritual maturity.**

James opens by telling his readers about the difficulties of life—and the life choices they will face in a variety of circumstances. No matter what difficulties we encounter, may God grant us "pure joy" in the midst of these difficulties, so that we may one day reach spiritual maturity. The joy we will experience is much greater than a mere feeling of happiness; it is a deep contentment in God's purpose for us, and it will grow stronger the closer we draw to Him.

How can we live as "a servant of God and of the Lord Jesus Christ" (James 1:1) in the world?

What is your normal reaction to trials and difficulties in life? How do James's words challenge you to respond in future?

Day 2

Read James 1:5–8

James now jumps from encouraging endurance to asking God for wisdom. Although this seems abrupt, it is characteristic of James's style.

James is not writing to address the specific issues of a church in turmoil, as Paul often does. Instead, he is consolidating a lifetime of serving the Lord into a short book on wisdom. We might say that this wisdom is "applied wisdom," in that James's goal is to spur his readers to action. It is likely that he regularly preached these ideas about wise living as part of longer messages during his earlier public ministry.

In fact, the jump is not as great as it may seem. James concludes his encouragement on endurance by noting that this trait leads to our being complete, "not lacking anything" (James 1:4). Then he says, "If any of you lacks wisdom . . ." (v. 5). He is making the point that troubles in life, dealt with in faith, will produce endurance leading to spiritual maturity—a full and meaningful life. But he does not stop there; he adds that even with the fullness of a mature faith, we will still need wisdom to continue to grow in Christ and to face *future* trials. James is moving from a general principle about growing in Christ to a reminder that this growth never stops. This is how he weaves his themes together.

When we face trials in life, they will increase our endurance and therefore our faith—for when we need wisdom to move forward, we will have to ask God. God will give wisdom "generously" to us "without finding fault" in our need or request (v. 5). Here, James is being consistent with the rest of the Bible, which teaches that wisdom comes from God first (e.g., Proverbs 2:6) and only secondarily from age or experience.

However, James has one clear warning about asking God for wisdom. We "must believe and not doubt" (James 1:6). Is it possible to be without doubt? When we use this word today, we link it to mixed feelings about our faith. James, however, is using an uncommon word in the original language, which means "to hesitate out of uncertainty." **He is *not* saying that we cannot receive wisdom if we are conflicted between earthly and heavenly things; rather, he is saying that if we cannot make up our minds about wanting wisdom, then we will not receive it.** We must go to God and ask without hesitation or second thoughts.

If we have second thoughts and are not committed to receiving wisdom from God, then our hesitation will cause us to go back and forth "like a wave of the sea" (1:6). We will be "double-minded"—literally of two minds—and "unstable" (1:8), because we will not be able to choose between what God's wisdom tells us and what our own sense of "wisdom" tells us.

The bad news is, we will always face trials. The good news is, God is always ready to give us the wisdom to face these trials and grow in our faith. And the great news is, He gives generously!

ThinkThrough

In what life circumstances do we need wisdom from God? How might wisdom help us cope?

When you think of asking God for wisdom, what kinds of hesitation arise in your heart and mind? How can we deal with them?

Day 3

Read James 1:9–11

Just as it is possible for a believer to be of two minds, so too it is possible for a believer to be of two circumstances in life: "humble circumstances" and "rich" (James 1:9–10). Here, James contrasts the rich and the poor—not just any rich and any poor, but rich believers and poor believers.

First, he tells the believers in humble circumstances that they can boast because their circumstances have put them in a "high position" (v. 9). While this seems opposite to the way the world works, James will later make the meaning of this "high position" clear.

Second, he tells the believers who are rich that their boasting will be due to their "humiliation," which will come when they "pass away like a wild flower" (v. 10). In a time before bright artificial colors were invented, ancient writers like James used wildflowers to paint a vivid image of a joyful burst of color in spring that quickly faded away with the arrival of summer (e.g., Job 14:2; Psalm 103:15; Isaiah 40:6; 1 Peter 1:24). In the original language, James is likening the rich to a "flower of the grass."

We don't usually think of a flower as having a low position; it may even be the high point of a walk in the garden. But an untended wildflower that springs up will only too quickly wither away. As the sun rises and time passes, its beauty will fade. The flower is brought low because while it was once beautiful—or perhaps thought itself beautiful among the grass—its beauty is not permanent.

The rich person is like that wildflower. People will notice the flower for a short time and think it beautiful, but the wildflower doesn't realize that the demise of its beauty is coming quickly. In the same way, those who boast in their riches cannot see that those riches will wither away. The rich will lose their wealth before they know it, and when the full light of day shines on them, they will be humbled and shown to be what they truly are—nothing more than a grass of the field, just like everyone else. The rich are no better than the poor.

What, then, is the "high position" (James 1:9) that those in humble circumstances may boast in? **Perhaps their lack of pride in wealth that frees them to exalt God without exalting themselves.** May we put our hope in the riches of God's grace—His care, concern, and commitment—in our lives, regardless of our finances!

Financial status often divides people. However, in what ways are poor and rich believers alike? What do the rich and poor in Christ have in common?

When God blesses believers with material riches, what should they do? What should they *not* do?

Day 4

Read James 1:12

In this short saying, James comes back to the issue of facing trials as a believer. He continues to interweave his primary topics throughout his letter, returning again and again to key issues and linking them to secondary ones.

James pronounces believers "blessed" if they are able to endure in their faith while facing trials (James 1:12). Earlier, we learned that perseverance is a necessary result of living a life of faith in this world, and in turn it helps to make our faith full and complete. We also learned that a believer who perseveres through trials would be made "mature and complete" (v. 4). Now we learn that such a believer is blessed as well. Why are we also blessed if we endure through trials in faith?

Those who endure trials are blessed because once they have survived the trials of life, they will receive "the crown of life that the Lord has promised to those who love him" (v. 12). This crown of life represents the reward given to those who endure in faith to the end (see Revelation 2:10). More accurately, in the original language, James is saying that the crown of life is promised to those who *keep on loving* God through the trials of life.

On his first pass at handling trials (Day 2), James said that endurance creates a fullness and completeness of faith. When he comes back to the issue, we learn that a believer's endurance not only completes his faith, but also earns him a crown as a sign of his fulfilment of life in Christ. **The crown is the believer's triumph that reveals to the world that his faith, which is growing in maturity, will one day be full and complete.**

Should believers congratulate themselves on their future crown? No. The triumph is a gift from God that results from His promises to people, revealed primarily in the sacrifice and gift of Jesus Christ. Believers must still endure in faith to the end of their lives, something that must never be taken lightly.

What types of trials cause one to be blessed? What types do not?

What parts of your life have been tested and proven genuine?

Day 5

Read James 1:13–15

When we encounter trials and temptations in life, we may wonder if it is God who tempts us in order to test us. Do all the struggles we face start with Him?

James leads off with a clear response: God is not tempting you. To explain, he walks his readers through the origin and process of temptation in the life of believers.

There are two things we need to know about God. First, He "cannot be tempted by evil" (James 1:13). In other words, the evil in this world has no sway or effect on Him. God is good, and He cannot deviate from His goodness. Second, God does not tempt anyone. Since He is good all the time without deviation, there is no evil that He can use to tempt people. It is outside the nature of God to tempt people. He is *unable* to do it.

Yet temptation does occur in a believer's life. James tells us that temptation starts with our "own evil desire" (v. 14). This is important: *Our temptations in life start with us longing for something.* When we see something we are tempted by, we may think that the temptation comes from outside of ourselves—from the object of our desire—but it does not.

It comes from the inside. Once the longing is created in our hearts, we are "dragged away" by its power and "enticed" (v. 14). **We create the temptation in our hearts that we are subsequently enslaved to!**

James uses the image of childbirth to illustrate how temptation grows. Once desire has started, it continues to grow within us; and it becomes sin when we start acting on it. Once this sin has a place in our lives, it will continue to hurt us until it consumes us. This is the process by which temptation can lead to our downfall and defeat as believers, if it is left unchecked.

God is not a tempter, but we are. We tempt others and we also tempt ourselves. This temptation-to-sin cycle, if not broken, will consume us and destroy us. Implied in James's warning is the means to break this cycle: recognize where the temptation is coming from, and block it in our hearts before it takes root. Since God is not tempted and is greater than us, He can help us with our temptations—we should be turning to Him if we are single-minded about overcoming temptation!

ThinkThrough

Think about the things you want. How might these wants lead to temptation?

How can we guard our lives from temptation?

Day 6

Read James 1:16–18

Where do good things come from? Our own ingenuity and hard work? Or do good things start from somewhere outside of ourselves?

James warns us not to be deceived into thinking that we are wise enough or good enough to provide for our own needs and solve our own problems. Instead, we must recognize that anything that is truly good for us starts with God. It comes down to us from heaven. In the original language, James's warning is worded in such a way as to catch the reader's attention (James 1:16).

When James refers to "every good and perfect gift" (v. 17), the poetry of his words in the original language leads some scholars to think that he was using a popular expression from his own time.[1] The expression probably meant that receiving a gift was always wonderful. If so, James is modifying this saying to add the disclaimer that this is true *only* of gifts that come from God. This is because gifts that come from above are always greater than those on earth. **People may not always give each other good gifts, but God gives only good gifts.**

Next, James explains why we can trust in the good gifts from God: it is because of His divine nature. God is the creator of the universe (Genesis 1), and like the sun and the stars He always shines bright. He is not like our world (see Numbers 23:19; Malachi 3:6), which is one of dusks and dawns—shadows that shift over time. On Earth, the light and shadows of day and night are fickle, but the light of the sun and stars themselves does not change. On Earth, the gifts of people are often fickle; but the gifts of God are always good.

James reminds us that one of the good gifts God has given us is to be set free from our past and reborn into new life by the truth of Jesus's life and death. This is the "birth" we experience when we first commit ourselves to Jesus's message (James 1:18). This was accomplished solely by God's will, based upon His sovereign right as ruler of the universe. This means that we get to be the "firstfruits" of what God is doing in our universe (v. 18). As believers in Christ, we are the recipients of God's best and sweetest gifts.

[1] For discussion of these points involving the text in the original language, see Peter H. Davids, *The Epistle of James: A Commentary on the Greek Text*, New International Greek Testament Commentary (Grand Rapids: Eerdmans).

What good things has God given you?

What responsibility do we have as the "firstfruits of all he created" (James 1:18)?

Day 7

Read James 1:19–21

Again, James starts his next bit of wisdom with an attention-catching, "Take note, dear Christians!"

Of what are we to take note? James fuses three significant proverbial ideas from the Old Testament and Jewish literature into a summary statement for those following the wisdom of God: "Everyone should be quick to listen, slow to speak and slow to become angry" (James 1:19). These three ideas—quick to listen, slow to speak, and slow to anger—are of prime importance in much of James's experience with living a God-honoring lifestyle. Let's consider each of them in turn.

First, James challenges us to make haste with our listening and not with our speech. As we go through life, there will be many times when someone says something negative, inflammatory, or condescending, and our natural tendency is to be very quick to respond—similar to "an eye for an eye," we are quick to give a hurtful remark for a hurtful remark. God's wisdom, however, tells us to jump to listen rather than jump to speak (see Proverbs 29:20; Ecclesiastes 5:2).

Second, when we do speak, we should pause and measure our words carefully. If we are to do as Jesus asks and really love people as God does, then we must consider how our words can show love and respect to others. Even when our words need to be strong, if we slowly think them through first, we will be far more effective at producing good fruit through them.

Third, as a result of being quick to listen, we will become slow to speak, and thus slow to anger. The anger James refers to is likely the kind that simmers and boils, encouraging retaliation against others.

While James did not mean this as a step-by-step process for living wisely, these ideas are closely related. **Once a person turns to anger, the attitude it creates in his life is hostile to "the righteousness that God desires" (James 1:20).**

Curiously, James writes "therefore" to show that verse 21 is the correct response to the problem of anger. He tells believers to get rid of all "moral filth and the evil that is so prevalent", and to accept the Word of God that has taken residence in our hearts—the Word that saves us, both from our sinfulness in general and our day-to-day struggle with anger specifically. We are to take note of this to grow in our faith and continue in wise living!

What are some ways in which we can practice being "quick to listen" (James 1:19)?

How can anger damage our lives?

Day 8

Read James 1:22–25

Though the words of Scripture are planted in believers, James warns us that there is still a danger of hearing it and then thinking that the mere act of hearing is sufficient. James is clear: If we hear biblical teaching and do not act on it, then we have deceived ourselves. **We must listen *and* obey. One is not enough.**

It is still possible for us to merely hear the Word of God today. We may go to church and listen to the pastor read from the Bible and exhort us to a changed life—but leave the church forgetting what we have heard. This was also a great concern in the ancient world. James was surely aware of the crowds of people who heard Jesus but wandered away, ignoring His calls to action (see John 6:66).

To make his point, James uses an analogy of a man who looks at himself in a mirror but cannot recall what he looks like afterward (James 1:23–25). If we hear God's Word but do not obey it, then we are like this man. In the ancient world, glass mirrors were less common than today, but most people had access to at least a bit of polished metal. More importantly, a mirror was a greater symbol of self-consideration than it is today.

When James speaks of the man who looks in the mirror and then forgets, he is implying that this man's thoughts and wisdom are shallow. His looking in the mirror has no effect.

James then explains that when we look to God's instructions for our lives and act on them—and continue to act on them—then God will bless us as a result of our obedience (v. 25). The one who takes a long, hard look at God's instructions for life, tries to keep them in mind, and does what they are saying, doesn't forget what these instructions look like. Because his actions will change who he is—and who he appears to be in the world.

When we obey God and follow His wisdom for our lives, we will be blessed in what we do (v. 25).

When we hear the Word, how can we know what God wants us to do? How can we be sure that we are hearing God's instructions and not our own? What practical steps do we need to take?

What does the Bible tell us we are to do in order to receive blessings from God? What are a few practical steps we can take to receive these blessings?

Day 9

Read James 1:26–27

What is religion? What does it mean to be religious?

This question is as important today as it was in James's day. James wrote about wisdom to believers who were "scattered among the nations" (James 1:1). These believers encountered a wide variety of worldviews, philosophies, and rituals that existed under the banner of "religion" (e.g., Acts 17:16–23). However, just because an idea or practice is described as religious does not mean that it honors God. For example, some of the people in James's day believed that it was a religious duty to make offerings to the emperor. This kind of act might gain a person social favor, but it does not honor God—in fact, it is "worthless" (James 1:26).

To explain a key application of wisdom—listening and speaking—James ties it to the practice of religion that is "pure and faultless" (v. 27). Here's James's point: if a person avoids making offerings to a king and claims to honor God alone, yet does not keep a tight rein on his tongue, that person has fooled himself (v. 26). Anyone who cannot control his words is not able to live in a way that honors God. **Blessing God on Sunday and cursing man on Monday is an inconsistent lifestyle—it leads nowhere.**

Perhaps James makes this point because he knows people who think they can do just that.

James now gives two examples of "religion that God our Father accepts," with the first being "to look after orphans and widows in their distress" (v. 27). This example is a tangible way to show love to others. In the ancient world, few cared about orphans and widows (see Isaiah 1:17), and there were no official support systems for such people.

The second example is "to keep oneself from being polluted by the world" (James 1:27). "Polluted" refers to sin, our brokenness, but in a religious sense. We are not to allow the rituals and customs of the world to become ours. For example, we are not to make offerings to emperors even if it is culturally expected. We are to keep ourselves close to God—and God alone.

James's two examples echo the two principles of the Great Commandment (Matthew 22:37–40). By God's grace, we are to love others, even unimportant people such as widows and orphans; and we are to love God, especially by keeping ourselves from sinful activities. These examples of the Great Commandment in action introduce the next few sections of the book of James.

Religion that is "pure and faultless" (James 1:27) becomes a part of our lives when we obey God's commands. Plenty of people in the world are religious—but their religion is not pure if it arises from their own sense of right and wrong. We show by our restraint and good works that our religion is real and is one that truly honors God.

What are other examples of "pure and faultless" religion?

How does "pure and faultless" religion relate to wisdom?

Day 10

Read James 2:1–4

Religion that is "pure and faultless" involves tangible expressions of loving others and loving God (James 1:26–27). Starting in Chapter 2, James develops further examples of how we are to live in order to love others.

One way is avoiding "favoritism" (2:1). Here, favoritism refers to privileging those who appear to have wealth and power over those who do not. James says that we are to avoid favoritism because we are "believers in our glorious Lord Jesus Christ" (v. 1). We are not to be partial to others, just as Christ was not partial in His treatment of us. Christ's sacrifice was made for all who believe, not just a privileged few (John 3:16; Romans 5:6–8).

After James establishes the principle and the rationale, he then suggests a hypothetical situation that believers may face. In this scenario, two people enter a church, fellowship, or other Christian gathering; one is "wearing a gold ring and fine clothes" and the other is "in filthy old clothes" (James 2:2). If, seeing this, we offer the one with nice clothes a special seat up front but tell the one with shabby clothes to stand in the back, we would be showing partiality based on external appearances. If we do that, James says, we would have become like a biased judge who stacks the scales to favor one party over another (v. 4).

There are two implications of James's wisdom. First, we cannot privilege some over others. All believers hold an equal place among each other before God. Just as the Bible condemns unjust scales (Proverbs 20:23), it also condemns unjust treatment of others (see Leviticus 19:15, Exodus 23:3).

Second, we cannot make assumptions based on the way people appear. In James's scenario, since the two people are guests, all we know about them is how they are dressed. But external features can be deceiving. God considers the internal, not the external, and we should be very careful to do likewise (Matthew 23:25–26).

Does this mean it would be right to give the poor person the nice seat and make the rich person stand in the back? This may sound just, but it would also make us stack the scales in favor of one party over the other. **Every age has different views of what seems right, but if we want to honor God, then we must hold on to His wisdom, not the world's (1 Corinthians 1:20).**

Even though all this is hypothetical, it is a common-enough scenario that can apply in many situations. The circumstances may change, but the principle—do not show favoritism—remains. We can rejoice that no matter who we are or where we come from, we will all receive an equal seat in God's house.

What situations have you found yourself in when you were tempted to show favoritism?

In what ways does God avoid showing favoritism? How does God show grace and love to all people?

Day 11

Read James 2:5–7

Again James seeks to build a close rapport with his audience, writing to them to "listen" and calling them "dear brothers and sisters" (James 2:5; see also v. 1). He then continues his discussion on how to treat rich and poor with a series of four questions (vv. 5–7).

In the oral culture of James's time, ancient writers frequently put sets of questions like these to audiences. We may be tempted to skip the multiple questions, but James asks us to consider each one in our hearts. Be forewarned: James is not asking us these questions in a neutral way. Instead, he is using an ancient style of rhetoric to encourage us to agree.

In the first question, James wants us to consider whether or not God has chosen the poor to be "rich in faith" and to "inherit the kingdom" (v. 5; see Matthew 5:3). While this reflects Jesus's teaching, we still may ask: Why do the poor merit such value in the eyes of God? Practically speaking, people who are materially poor tend to have fewer distractions and a greater need to rely on God (see Matthew 19:24). In some ways, poverty can be good for the soul.

After this question, James interjects, "But you have dishonored the poor" (James 2:6). This short clause notes that

when we show favoritism, we dishonor those who have found favor with God. There is a twist here: in the first half of verse 6, James refers to "you" as the one dishonoring the poor (such as making them stand in the back); but in the second half of verse 6, he asks his readers to consider whether or not the rich are hurting "you." Is James saying that his readers mistreat the poor even though they are poor themselves? How ironic, if believers who are poor hurt other poor people!

In the early Christian world, "poor" and "rich" often took on meanings beyond the simple measure of material wealth. Rich meant "honored," though it also implied being corrupt. Conversely, poor not only meant "no money," but also meant "dishonorable and despised," and in some cases could even imply freedom from corrupt society. Many early Christians lacked money, but they wanted to avoid worldly corruption. Therefore, all believers are to avoid dishonoring the poor through their cultural attitudes toward poverty and wealth.

Questions two through four are closely tied together (vv. 6–7). Their goal is to push us into seeing the error of our actions. In the ancient world, the rich often treated the poor cruelly, and most believers at that time were poor. Therefore, whether rich or poor, believers cannot accept the way society treats the poor.

Whether we are ourselves poor or rich, we should strive to treat each other equally and see the value in all people. This value does not come from within; it comes from our Creator, the God who gives us life, hope, and wisdom. We love others because He created others in His image (Genesis 1:27).

ThinkThrough
_____

How does the way we are treated by those wealthier and more powerful than us shape the way we see our world? When we see injustice, how should we respond?

How can we better minister to those in our community who are in need?

Day 12

Read James 2:8–11

After noting the problem of favoritism (Day 10, James 2:1–4) and the ironies that come with it (Day 11, vv. 5–7), James moves on to show from Scripture why favoritism is wrong. As a Christian, it is not enough to feel that an action or attitude is wrong; we should also look to Scripture to determine how to live. This is what James does now.

James builds his argument from Scripture in four steps: a good possibility, a bad possibility, a principle that supports these possibilities, and an example that supports the principle.

The good possibility (James 2:8): If we can keep the "royal law" in the Bible ("Love your neighbor as yourself"), we will be making good choices in our lives. It's only a possibility, because loving my neighbor as myself is not easy! But if we can do it, then we can really do good with our lives. Yet James implies that fully keeping this law is impossible, because we will always encounter situations in life when we need to love our neighbors to a greater degree than we do now.

Why does James call this the "royal law"? He is most likely echoing the teachings of Jesus. During His public ministry, Jesus used the terms "kingdom of God" and" kingdom of heaven" to help people understand how God was moving in the world. Loving our neighbor as ourselves is not just the "greatest commandment" (Matthew 22:37–40), but also the foundation for kingdom-living. It is a hallmark of what God is pushing us toward.

The bad possibility (James 2:9): In contrast with living for our King, there is also a risk that we may be tempted toward worldliness and showing partiality. If we choose this bad option, then we sin, and in the eyes of God we would be "law-breakers."

The principle (James 2:10): James supports the conclusion of the bad possibility—that favoritism is a criminal offense against God's rule—by explaining that a person who breaks only one part breaks the entire law. Unlike many modern legal systems, in which each law stands on its own merit, God's law comes from God himself, and is all or nothing—as is the loyalty that we are to show to God. This idea is reflected in Jesus's saying that not even the smallest part of the law will disappear until it is completed (Matthew 5:18).

The example (James 2:11): Finally, James offers an example to defend his principle. If you obey one law (against adultery) but break another (against murder), you have still broken the law of God.

There are two kinds of wisdom—one that leads to "royal" behavior, and one that leads to "criminal" behavior. **If we show favoritism, we are following worldly wisdom and rebelling against God's plan.** The good news is, God generously gives us the right kind of wisdom if we ask, so that we may honor Him throughout our lives.

ThinkThrough

Why are God's laws so important? Why are they more important than human laws? Why must we keep God's laws above all else?

How can we avoid being "law break-ers" (James 2:9) as we try to live in a world that constantly shows favoritism?

Day 13

Read James 2:12–13

James's final thoughts about the sin of showing partiality toward the rich over the poor take the form of a general calling for believers in Christ about the way we are to live in relation to God and others. He tells his readers pointedly, "[so you] speak and [so you] act as those who are going to be judged by the law that gives freedom" (James 2:12). In writing this way, he is emphasizing both the words and the actions of the believer.

In what way are we to talk and live?

We are to talk and live as if God's great future for us is now. If we are in Christ, we will one day be judged by the law of Christ. But this law liberates, because it is a law that judges us not on what we say and do, but on our relationship to Christ. We are lawbreakers, and if we are judged by the law apart from Christ, we will be found guilty. But if we are bound to Christ, we are judged with Christ. We cannot be double-minded in the way we speak and act.

Therefore, since we have been freed by Christ and will one day be judged as such, **we are to talk and live as if we have already been judged free.** We are to speak and act in full anticipation of our glorification. We are to speak and act as full members of the kingdom of heaven.

If we don't, James notes, there is a consequence. When we show partiality to the rich and dishonor the poor, we are not showing mercy to the poor. We are judging them with our worldly wisdom and lack of godly compassion (v. 4). If we are not merciful to those in need, we face consequences when He judges us.

James concludes with a proverb, a reminder, a shout-out for us: "Mercy triumphs over judgment" (v. 13)! God's mercy is proclaimed over God's judgment; when we show mercy, we proclaim the greatness of God far more than when we judge others.

Let us speak and show love to others without partiality and with mercy, liberally applied.

What is one practical way of living as people redeemed by the gospel? How can we show to others that we are not double-minded about our life with God?

In what situations can we show mercy even when we are tempted to judge?

Day 14

Read James 2:14–17

Today we cover the most well-known assertion in the book of James: "Faith by itself, if it is not accompanied by action, is dead" (James 2:17).

A superficial reading of the verse incorrectly implies that works lead to salvation. As a result, so much has been written on this verse over the past 2,000 years that it often clouds this section of James and overshadows the entire book. This is unfortunate, because what James weaves together is not only compelling and crucial but also fully resonant with the rest of Scripture.

James opens with two questions for his readers to consider (v. 14). The first aims to get his readers thinking deeply about the relationship between faith and deeds. By "faith," James means a person's internal commitment to God. By "deeds," he means a person's external activities, done in obedience to God's commands. James asks the reader to speculate *if it is possible* for a person to have internal commitment but no external sign of that commitment. The second question is, *if it is possible* to have such a faith, is that faith sufficient for right standing with God?

By starting this way, James is signalling to the reader that this is a difficult topic. There is a tension between faith and deeds that encourages us to see the relationship between the two—and not to choose between them.

Next, James offers an example to encourage deeper reflection on the opening questions. In this scenario, we meet another believer on the street who is "without clothes and daily food" (v. 15). Again, James raises a hypothetical question: What good does it do to harbor good feelings inside for that person and to voice such feelings out loud, but not do anything to address their immediate needs? In other words, what happens to that believer when we have an internal commitment to them, but do not show any tangible, external sign of our commitment?

The point of James's hypothetical puzzle for us is this: if we say we care about a destitute person, how much do we really care if we do not also act on it? Care for others that we feel but don't act on isn't really care. In the same way, James is suggesting, if we care about God internally but do not show it externally, that care goes nowhere. It is dead. So, if we claim to be a follower of Christ and claim to have an internal commitment to God, but we show no external sign of that commitment, then it must be "dead" (v. 17). **Works are thus the external evidence of a real internal faith.**

James was well aware that Jesus had encountered people who said they believed but struggled to act on it (see Matthew 19:16–26). He understood that the doing, while hard, is what makes our believing come alive. May we commit our lives to action in Jesus's name, so our faith in Him comes alive!

Where do you see tension between belief and action in your life? How can you ensure that your actions come from real faith?

Why do you think James includes hypothetical situations instead of just telling us plainly what to do?

Day 15

Read James 2:18–26

James now tackles objections he predicts will be raised to his statement on faith and works (Day 14, James 2:14–17). This involves a series of examples and questions.

The primary objection that James predicts is the argument that faith and deeds are valid individually; they can be split among people, similar to gifts (v. 18). As if this were possible! James teases his challenger, suggesting that he shows his "faith without deeds" (v. 18). Since faith is an internal commitment, how can one demonstrate it outwardly if not through deeds? In short, one cannot. Thus, James is telling his opponent that because he has genuine faith, he can demonstrate faith externally—by his actions. **People demonstrate real faith through loving action.**

James points out that his challenger may have accurate theology—belief in one God (v. 19). But he then uses hyperbole to suggest that even the worst creatures—demons—have "good theology" in that regard, as they too believe in one God. Yet demons do not have commitment to that one God, nor do they engage in good works because of Christ's sacrifice.

Calling his hypothetical challenger "foolish" (v. 20), James then raises another series of questions. While the readers of his letter are not his challengers, James uses a rhetorical strategy to put his readers in the midst of the debate.

The questions revolve around two examples. First, the deeds of Abraham (vv. 21–24). James asks whether it was the actions of Abraham—his willingness to sacrifice Isaac—that made him righteous (see Hebrews 11:17). James's next statement is perhaps his most important: "You see that his faith and his actions were working together, and his faith was made complete by what he did" (James 2:22). James is not arguing for works alone nor downplaying the importance of faith. Rather, he is explaining that faith and works are two parts of the same whole in a person who is truly following Christ.

Second, the deeds of Rahab the prostitute (vv. 25–26). James asks whether it was the actions of Rahab—risking her life to give assistance to the enemy—that made her righteous. The answer is clear. Rahab's action was an expression of her faith (Joshua 2:9–11). With the example of Abraham (man, patriarch of Israel) and Rahab (woman, foreigner), James shows that faith must be accompanied by deeds for *all* believers.

James's prediction of challenges to his explanation of the relationship between faith and works echoes Jesus's critique of the Pharisees (e.g., Matthew 12:33–37). A challenger may argue that correct beliefs are merely enough to please God. If that were true, would that also mean that correct works are merely enough to please God?

In order to please God, you must believe and do (Deuteronomy 11:26–28). Right doing starts with right believing, and right believing is evidenced by right doing. Today, let us answer James's hypothetical question with our lives—living both with faith in Christ and deeds for Christ.

Why do accurate beliefs only go so far?

How can we check our faith against our works? What about our works against our faith?

Day 16

Read James 3:1–6

James 3:1 signals a new topic with the introduction "My fellow believers." The author now turns the readers' attention to how our words affect our lives. As usual, he mixes issues, proverbs, and examples together to encourage his readers.

In reading James's first statement, we get a distinct sense that he was worried about too many people pushing to become teachers too quickly. In the ancient world, a teacher was often seen as a leader, and the position carried more authority than it does today; a "teacher" then may have been more like "pastor" or "professor" now. Since people were seeking the position whether they were qualified or not, James warns that "we who teach will be judged more strictly" (v. 1).

It is not clear what prompted his concerns. Were there increasing numbers of teachers who taught inaccurately? Or were there increasing numbers of teachers who knew the material intellectually, but whose words showed them to be immature or hypocritical? Both of these scenarios would have damaged kingdom growth. Teaching others, especially in spiritually critical situations such as a Bible study or sermon, should not be undertaken lightly. James quickly adds, however, that no one is perfect. If it were possible for someone to always speak well, that person would be perfect (v. 2)! Next we have three examples that flesh out James's concerns about speaking and teaching. In his letter, the word "tongue" (v. 5) is used to depict our way of speaking to others.

First, James compares our tongue to the metal bits placed in the mouths of horses to control them (v. 3). Second, he compares our tongue to the rudders of large ships (v. 4). The point he is making in both cases is that a small object (the tongue, bit, or rudder) directs a much larger object (the person, horse, or ship). In other words, just as a small rudder can steer a big ship the wrong way, so too can a small word from a person's mouth steer that person the wrong way, such as through "great boasts" (v. 5). **Speaking carelessly and hurtfully to others steers our lives toward sin.**

Third, James compares our tongue to the spark that starts a huge fire (v. 5). The point he is making is that even though the spark itself may be small, the damage it causes is extensive. He also notes that the tongue becomes like this fire, but the fire of the tongue does not just harm others—it also consumes the speaker (v. 6)!

Our temptation to boast and speak poorly of others starts from our sinfulness. If we speak evil, it is like a fire that "corrupts the whole body" (v. 6); it engulfs us in flames and destroys the trajectory of our lives. It is a challenge to always speak well, but one that we believers must undertake.

Why is the tongue so damaging in our relationships with others? What about with God?

What are some concrete or practical steps we can take to prevent our tongues from controlling us?

Day 17

Read James 3:7–8

As Christians, we should never underestimate the power of our words to harm others and ruin ourselves. Our tongue is like the bit in a horse's mouth or the rudder of a ship—a small, simple thing that controls the direction of the whole entity—and it is like a fire that can consume our lives (James 3:3–6). Its power is deceptive because it seems so small, yet it causes so many problems.

To illustrate this, James points out that "all kinds of animals, birds, reptiles and sea creatures" have been tamed and to this day can still be tamed by mankind (v. 7), thus reminding readers of humanity's general dominion over the world. Yet even though people have dominion over the world and can subdue all kinds of animals, no person can subdue his own tongue (v. 8)!

This last illustration by James is the most extreme, though it may not be obvious to modern readers. In the ancient world, subduing an animal meant approaching it on foot with a weapon in hand. Only great heroes could subdue wild beasts, an extremely dangerous task. But even the greatest hero cannot subdue the little thing in his mouth.

The reason, James reveals, is that the tongue "is a restless evil, full of deadly poison" (v. 8). The explanation for why the tongue is untameable is suggested in the word "restless," which is the same word as "unstable" in James 1:8, where the "double-minded" man is described. The tongue is "restless" in that it is often used without forethought, purpose, or logic.

The tongue of a person is entirely unpredictable. It is out of control, which is why it is untameable. It is a poison, a corrupting influence that, if we are not careful, will be the means of our destruction.

Remember, James's point so far is not that our tongues burn other people or poison larger communities (though that is also true; see Proverbs 12:18; 15:1); his point is that our tongues burn and poison *ourselves*. And once they burn us, they then go on to burn others (James 3:5).

Our modern society permits people to use their tongues in unwise ways—ways that people in authority in the ancient world would not have tolerated. As a result, our situation today is even more dire than when James was writing; we can do a great deal of damage with our tongues, but the consequences are delayed.

As believers, however, our call is to possess real faith and real deeds, and the first and most obvious deed that will reflect Christ in our lives is to bring our tongues into obedience to God.

ThinkThrough

How have you experienced the unpredictable poison of the tongue?

What are some practical steps we can take to limit the damage our tongues can do?

Day 18

Read James 3:9–12

The logical end of James's warning about the tongue is this: just as Christians cannot be double-minded (1:8), we cannot be double-tongued either. With our tongues "we praise our Lord and Father, and with it we curse human beings"; when both good and bad come from our lips, it makes us duplicitous (James 3:9; see also Proverbs 10:32).

"My brothers and sisters, this should not be" (James 3:10). But it is much harder to keep our words single-minded than we think.

Praising God is perhaps the supreme thing a person can do with the lips. We can speak directly to—and worship—the creator of the universe.

Cursing others, on the other hand, is perhaps the foulest way to use our words. Since people are made in the image of God, cursing them is cursing something that God created. When we are out and about, and some random person does us wrong, it is tempting to speak ill of him or her—but we would be speaking ill of a creation patterned after God himself. We must always keep God's perspective of people in mind, not reacting out of anger or hurt.

James offers two illustrations of why good and bad speech are irreconcilable in the life of the Christian. First, he asks his readers whether it is possible for fresh water and salt water to come from the same source (v. 11). Second, he asks his readers whether it is possible for a fig tree to produce olives, or for a grapevine to yield figs (v. 12). The answer he wants his readers to arrive at for each of his questions is this: "No. It is not possible."

James's point is that a water source can produce either fresh water or salt water, but not both. **If we are believers, our tongues must not emit both blessings and curses; instead, they should produce crops in accordance with where our hearts lie.** Here, James is reflecting the words of Jesus (see Matthew 7:16–18).

Just as there are two kinds of wisdom that can flow out of our lives—that which comes from heaven and that which comes from earth—there are two kinds of talk that can come out of our mouths. We must choose one and avoid the other. They are not compatible, and they cannot coexist in our lives.

Why do you think the tongue is so duplicitous, speaking both good and bad?

Why is it difficult to see other people as made in the image of God?

Day 19

Read James 3:13–16

James asks his readers to think of someone they know who appears wise and knowledgeable (James 3:13). In fact, this someone may very well be one of his own readers! Then comes his advice—we can discover who is really wise and who is not by examining their motives.

If a person who claims to be wise has a humble spirit and leads a "good life" (v. 13), then this is a sign that his wisdom is true (see v. 17). But if a person who claims to be wise shows hints of jealousy or selfish ambition, be careful—this person likely has built his "wisdom" from an earthly, sinful source (vv. 14–15; see also Proverbs 3:7). **True wisdom is exemplified in our ministry to others and not in reward for ourselves.**

James speaks pointedly to his readers when he says: if you have envy or ambition, "do not boast about it or deny the truth" (James 3:14). In other words, if you read this thinking you have wisdom and understanding, but your life and actions are marked by jealousy and selfishness, then you must neither hide them nor be proud of them.

People who claim to be wise but have these flaws need to understand that the source of their wisdom is likely demonic (v. 15). The word

"demonic" may conjure up images of paranormal activity for us (and probably for James' readers as well), but James is in fact contrasting wisdom that comes from God and wisdom that comes from places in rebellion against God—earth and hell. These sources are at war with each other, and thus the two kinds of wisdom that come from them are at odds with each other.

The result of people being motivated by jealousy and selfish desire is the "disorder" and "evil practice" that follow in their wake (v. 16). Though these kinds of people may claim to be wise and knowledgeable, their personal lives are a mess—there is a clear trail of wreckage behind them.

James's readers would have likely been aware that true wisdom comes only from respecting and obeying God (Proverbs 1:7; 2:6; 9:10). In contrast, worldly wisdom can take many forms: age, experience, and education, for example. But there are really only two sources for the two kinds of wisdom.

Many people in our world today claim wisdom, but we should be circumspect of those claims. True wisdom is not claimed or earned, but given by God. We do well when we ask God to grant us wisdom to live in a way that honors Him.

ThinkThroug

Why are people
so quick to follow
someone who
claims wisdom and
knowledge?

What are several
practical examples
of true wisdom
today?

Read James 3:17–18

We are now at the heart of James's message: wisdom. For many people, the search for wisdom is key to earthly success. In the garden, Eve ate the fruit because she hoped to have wisdom and understanding without going through God (Genesis 3:6). Solomon asks for wisdom from God, and the request pleased God (1 Kings 3:9). Several books of the Bible address the issue of wisdom, most notably Proverbs.

In thinking about wisdom, James likely read how Solomon was unmatched in wisdom while young but later traded that wisdom for human foolishness. He was familiar with the development of wisdom in the writings of Proverbs, Ecclesiastes, and probably other Jewish works like Sirach (a popular book modelled on Proverbs and written 200 years before Jesus). James had heard his half-brother Jesus speak with wisdom.

What is wisdom? **Wisdom is the ability to effectively apply what we know whenever we need to act.** The most famous example is found in 1 Kings 3:16–28, where Solomon applies his understanding of the depth of a mother's love to determine how two people in conflict will act in a given situation. It is important to remember that from a biblical point of view, real wisdom does not come from age, experience, learning, or intelligence. Those things may produce a kind of wisdom, but it is not the same as real wisdom. Why? Because—the Bible makes this point repeatedly—real wisdom comes from God (e.g., Proverbs 1:7). As believers, we may possess a kind of wisdom from our experiences on earth, but what we really want and need is the real wisdom that comes only from God.

In 3:17–18, James helps his readers understand some characteristics of wisdom, so they can determine what kind of wisdom they see in others (and themselves).

First and foremost, godly wisdom is "pure," meaning it is holy and not lacking in anything (v. 17). Just as God is complete in himself, so too is His wisdom complete in itself. God's wisdom is sufficient (Matthew 4:4; Deuteronomy 8:3).

Godly wisdom is also "peace-loving, considerate, submissive, full of mercy and good fruit, impartial and sincere" (James 3:17). Notice how each of these qualities stand in contrast to wisdom motivated by envy and ambition (v. 14). If you see someone with these qualities, it is a sure sign that their wisdom comes from the Lord.

James concludes this section with a statement about peacemakers, who in this case would possess godly wisdom and know how to deal with the challenges James brings up in chapter 4. Amid the storms of life, these peacemakers calm others, which allows godliness to take root and grow.

As we live our lives, people will try to influence us, claiming to be wise and knowledgeable. We must be aware that there are two kinds of wisdom in this world—one we follow, and one we reject in order to avoid being double-minded (1:8). Let's ask God to grant us the wisdom we need to be faithful in all He has called us to do. He will give generously, as every good and perfect gift comes from Him (1:17).

ThinkThrough

In a world overflowing with knowledge, why is wisdom of critical importance today?

How can we discern the type of wisdom people are using in the world?

Day 21

Read James 4:1–3

James opens this section with two questions (James 4:1). The first is open-ended, encouraging his readers to think about why there are "fights and quarrels" (v. 1) even between fellow Christians. The second is closed, with no room for debate. It pushes his readers to admit something they would rather not: when strife occurs between others and us, it springs from the cravings within our own hearts. The "desires that battle within" (v. 1) us are signs of our double-mindedness; this is a struggle we all face.

These two questions set up the hypothetical scenarios that follow (v. 2). They contain some of the strongest words in James's work.

"You want something but don't get it."

"You covet, but you cannot have what you want, so you kill."

"You quarrel and fight."

In each of these scenarios, James implies that our selfishness does not lead to getting what we want but rather to dissatisfaction and discord. His use of "you" here is pointed. While we may be tempted to think he is addressing a specific situation at the time, James's letter is intended for a wider audience (1:1). These scenarios happen to all of us, whoever we may be.

Now James bites his readers with sarcasm—we don't have because we don't ask God (4:2). Yes, it is true that we should ask God for whatever we need, as He wants to provide for us. But is it really God's intent to provide the things for which we lust and covet? **The reason we want and don't receive is that our hearts are in the wrong place.** We are asking not out of need but out of selfish desire (v. 3). If our purpose is to please our unbridled passion and selfishness, God will not grant our request.

Again, James's words echo—and illuminate—what Jesus taught. God wants to help with our needs (Matthew 7:7–11). We are to approach Him boldly, believing that if we ask for what we need, He will give (21:22). In James's day, as in our own time, people heard Jesus's words and tried to apply them far outside their intent—praying for "needs" that benefited themselves, not others. We ask God to meet our needs *and* to meet the needs of others (5:42).

What are some examples of craving that can cause conflict in our lives?

How can we differentiate our wants from our needs, to better approach God?

We live in a world that encourages us to love and put ourselves first. The message of the Bible, seen here in James, is the opposite. To love others is greater than to love ourselves. Doing this is not easy, but it is God's plan, and He will give us the strength to see it through.

Day 22

Read James 4:4–6

Up to now, James has been addressing his readers warmly as "brothers and sisters" (James 1:2, 16, 19; 2:1, 5, 14; 3:10, 12). In this section, however, he coldly addresses them as "adulterous people" (4:4). These words seem harsh to us today, but James is not accusing his readers of sexual immorality; rather, he is following the Old Testament tradition of using adultery as a *dysphemism* (vulgar expression to make a point) to describe someone who has been unfaithful to God (see Jeremiah 3:8; Ezekiel 16:32).

Why would James switch to such sharp language? The root of the problem is that some of his readers have demonstrated "friendship with the world" (James 4:4). James is asking his readers whether they know that being friendly with the world (humanity's attempts to create their own society apart from God) is the same as hating God.

To our modern ears, this allegation might seem a bit extreme. The key, however, is in the word "friendship"—a word that has taken on numerous meanings today, especially with the rise of social media. To James and his readers, "friendship" would have meant "strong companionship" or even "allegiance."

James is not suggesting that those who have acquainted themselves (a weak relationship) with the world are haters of God. Rather, he is saying that if you ally yourself to the world (a strong relationship), your allegiance demonstrates a profound "enmity against God" (v. 4). Since people are a special creation of God, and He loves us, if people hate Him and unite with the world, they have shared themselves with the world and are "adulterous" in their union with God.

If you ally yourself with the world, you are an enemy of God; James does not suggest there is any middle ground. To defend his argument, he cites Scripture twice.

The first reference (v. 5) is not clear to us today, as it is a very difficult verse to translate. James could be trying to remind us that God is jealous for us, as His Spirit who lives in us compels Him to be that way. Or, he could be warning us that our human nature is full of selfishness, and this is what propels us toward an allegiance with the world. Either way, God's grace is greater (v. 6).

The second reference is from

Proverbs 3:34, which James adapts to emphasize that when we do not ally ourselves with the world but submit ourselves to God and His will for our lives, He will not oppose our work but in fact supports it through His great grace for us.

There is wisdom from the world, and there is wisdom from God. When we listen to God, we reject the world, and God, who is good, pours out His grace upon us. Let us break our allegiances to the world and recommit ourselves daily to the goodness of God.

ThinkThrough

How do we commit "adultery" toward God in our everyday lives?

What does it look like to "unfriend" the world?

Day 23

Read James 4:7–10

After several critical questions and answers that have surely put his readers on the defensive, James now changes his tone and speaks with encouragement about a series of expansive adjustments they can make to get their lives back on track (James 4:7–10). His words are almost melodic, as he uses similar phrasing for each one to enhance his rhetorical effect.

More than a list, these instructions are intended to be a course correction after the hard words that came before. With the help of the Spirit (v. 5), we are to do the following:

- Swear allegiance to God
- Resist temptations
- Grow in our relationship with God
- Renounce outwardly sinful deeds
- Repent inwardly for lack of allegiance
- Mourn what brought us to this point
- Get serious about our faith
- Surrender ourselves to God

Individually, each of these could be read, reflected on, and discussed at length by the readers of James's letter. Each one represents an important step for believers to take as they commit their lives to God. Yet it is also James's intent for us to hear them together, as one great, encouraging challenge calling his readers back to God. Together, they are part of a larger strategy for eliminating double-mindedness in our lives.

Together, these challenges amount to a deeply personal, deeply emotional call for readers to reconnect with God. The God we are to embrace tearfully is a living and faithful God (Genesis 28:15; Psalm 23)—an incredible contrast with what James's readers would have experienced with entirely stone-faced, impersonal idols (Habakkuk 2:18–19) or with a cold, uncaring world (Ecclesiastes 1:14; Ephesians 6:12). This is not a list of commands as much as a list of commitments. Only a God who is invested in us and who is faithful to the end, would encourage His people to this depth of commitment.

There are two kinds of wisdom in this world—one that says, "Make yourself king," and the other that says, "Submit yourself to the King." Yet, to *gain* true wisdom is really to *lose* one's self-established status and privilege by swearing allegiance to God. From there we leave our past with true sorrow and repentance, and become serious about our faith. May God grant us the heart and strength to do as James exhorts!

ThinkThrough

What emotions do James's list of challenges evoke in you?

Which of these challenges do you most or least resonate with, and why?

Day 24

Read James 4:11–12

After a more difficult subject, James switches back to the issue of how we are to speak to each other. To do this, he returns to a warmer form of address, with "brothers and sisters" (James 4:11).

James warns that we are not to "slander one another" (v. 11). Here, slander is described in two ways: first, it is saying ill or evil things about another believer; and second, it is passing judgment on a fellow Christian. James has noted this problem of the tongue before (3:8–9).

When we slander others, it goes beyond just hurting them. When we slander or judge others, it has two additional effects: first, we are speaking against God's rules for life (the law); and second, we are actually sitting in judgment over God's rules.

What this means is that when we attack others with our words, we are in effect taking God's role away from Him.

It is God's place to judge people, and His rules for life confirm this. To speak ill of others and judge their lives, therefore, suggests that we have made ourselves God. This idea is so crucial that one of the main epithets for the Enemy of God, Satan, is "devil," which means "slanderer."

Our modern world often misses the point of this passage. In criticizing slander and judgment of fellow believers, James is *not* against giving other believers loving but hard advice, or calling them away from a sinful path (see 5:19–20). He is not addressing the issue of tolerance, but the issue of condemnation. Jesus's words, "do not judge, or you too will be judged" (Matthew 7:1), which are so frequently misappropriated by our culture today, receive a welcome explanation in James's writing.

At issue is the person and nature of God. God is the only true "Lawgiver and Judge," and the only being who is able to both "save and destroy" (James 4:12). As creatures created by our Creator, it is incredibly important that we do not say or do anything that usurps His authority. When we slander and judge, however, we usurp God's authority, and this is why James ends with a pointed question: "But you—who are you to judge your neighbor?" (v. 12). The emphasis is on "you" and "who"; James is implying, "Do you think you are God himself?"

God has given us so much privilege in this life that we can be tempted to take over His authority. Instead, we should humble ourselves and honor

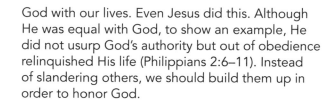

God with our lives. Even Jesus did this. Although He was equal with God, to show an example, He did not usurp God's authority but out of obedience relinquished His life (Philippians 2:6–11). Instead of slandering others, we should build them up in order to honor God.

Why are we tempted to slander other believers? What damage does slandering others do to them and ourselves?

Why do you think people in our world slander others? What does slander say about how we view ourselves and God?

Day 25

Read James 4:13–17

To encourage his readers to live with wisdom, James presents another hypothetical scenario for his readers to consider—a wasted life.

We are tempted to live in the moment and celebrate our accomplishments; to go through the motions at work, to enjoy the downtime, and to not worry much about the needs of others or even our own future (James 4:13). This temptation was as true in the ancient world as it is today.

"Futile" is James's response to that attitude. No one knows "what will happen tomorrow" (v. 14). Therefore, building plans solely based on immediate wants and interests is a bad idea. James poses an open-ended question (v. 14) to get his readers to think deeply about what their "life" even means. Then he tells them something no one wants to admit—our lives are here today, gone tomorrow.

"For who knows what is good for a person in life, during the few and meaningless days they pass through like a shadow?," says Solomon (Ecclesiastes 6:12). James agrees. Yet, even as people feel this way, God still has a plan for each of us.

There is an answer to this situation. **Instead of saying that we are going to go and do as we like (James 4:13), James suggests that we speak of our activities as predicated on God's will for our lives (v. 15).** This kind of godly humility serves as a sharp contrast to human arrogance.

At first, this may seem little more than a word game. What difference does it make if we say, "I'm moving to Antioch," versus saying, "If it is the Lord's will, I'm moving to Antioch?" James, however, feels that the difference is of critical importance to wise living.

First, if we simply speak of what we will do based on our own wishes, we are "boasting and bragging" about our own strength (v. 16). God is the one who has put us here, in this time and place, for a purpose; if we pretend this is not the case and speak of ourselves only—"*I* will do this and *I* will do that"—then we would be omitting God from His place in our lives. We would be speaking more highly of ourselves than we deserve.

Second, "all such boasting is evil" (v. 16). James does not say boasting is evil (though it may be), he says boasting *such as this* is evil. There is something evil about bragging about our lives as if God is not part of them. As Christians, we know that He desires to be intimately involved

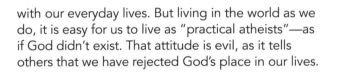

with our everyday lives. But living in the world as we do, it is easy for us to live as "practical atheists"—as if God didn't exist. That attitude is evil, as it tells others that we have rejected God's place in our lives.

James concludes: "If anyone, then, knows the good they ought to do and doesn't do it, it is sin for them" (v. 17). Not only is it evil for us to live as "practical atheists," but it is also sinful for us to live selfishly. When we live for ourselves, we waste opportunities to show God's love to others through our words and deeds.

ThinkThrough

How might our words and attitude suggest to others that God is not in charge of our lives?

How can we make sure we seek God and His will as we plan out our lives?

Day 26

Read James 5:1–6

James switches to another issue: wealth. Whereas we tend to group people into three categories—lower, middle, and upper class—thinkers and writers in the ancient world put them into only two groups: rich and poor.

Conventional wisdom suggests that in James's day, most people were poor—especially Christians. However, by the time John was writing Revelation, the Christians in Laodicea could go so far as to claim that their wealth had made them great (Revelation 3:17). While many of James's readers were poor, there were some who were materially rich. Many were also gaining some degree of financial influence in the "commercial class" economic boom caused by the spread of the Roman Empire[2]—though the elites still considered them poor. And many, while not materially wealthy, reflected the attitudes of the elite (see Day 11). James's warning was thus likely directed at both the rich as well as those who were in the process of becoming more wealthy or who behaved as if they were.

James grabs his readers' attention with, "Now listen!" (James 5:1). He is speaking to them in much the same way as he did in his other scenarios. If we are rich as James describes, then we had better be prepared to weep for the "misery" that is coming upon

us (v. 1). This warning is followed by a list of problems associated with those who are rich (vv. 2–6): your wealth has rotted; you have hoarded; you have failed to pay people; you have lived in indulgence; and you have condemned the innocent.

It is important to note that after listing these problems, James does not offer a simple summary on how to deal with wealth. Thus, we can interpret this to mean that wealth introduces a host of problems into a believer's life. As with much of James's words, he is reflecting the teachings of Jesus (v. 2, compare with Matthew 6:19–21). **Their argument does not appear to be that wealth itself is sinful, but that wealth exposes one to a great deal of sin.** Although not rich, many of James's readers would have found themselves with some wealth. James's words come across as a strong warning not to emulate the failures of the rich.

Many people today find themselves in a position where they do not feel wealthy but would still be considered rich by people who lived just a few generations ago. The attitudes that surround wealth are difficult to navigate in any generation. Though we ourselves may not feel wealthy, we must not follow the world's lead and think or act the way James warns us against. Whatever degree of material wealth we possess, our real treasure is in the spiritual gifts that God gives—so that we can bless those around us.

[2] Emanuel Mayer, *The Ancient Middle Classes: Urban Life and Aesthetics in the Roman Empire, 100 BCE–250 BCE* (Cambridge: Harvard University Press, 2012), 2.

ThinkThrough

How can wealth become a slow cancer that eats away at a person's spiritual life?

How can a person be "well-off" or "comfortable" in our world today, yet not fall into sin?

Day 27

Read James 5:7–11

To live in the light of heavenly—not earthly—wisdom requires us to be patient in the world we live in. As believers, we look to God to direct our days, not nurture our self-interests.

Speaking affirmatively to them as "brothers and sisters," James reminds his readers to be patient in waiting for the Lord's return (James 5:7). In the first century, believers thought that Jesus would likely return in their lifetimes; for us today, though we are not sure when Jesus will come back, we certainly wish He would return soon, so the message of patience applies to us as well.

James offers the example of the farmer who "waits for the land to yield its valuable crop" (v. 7). This analogy tells his original readers that if they are to go about their Father's business while waiting for Jesus's return, they will experience a great harvest from God. Again, the same thing is true for us today—we are to be patient as we wait for the work God does through us to turn into valuable crops. We are to wait for the rains that God will send to build His kingdom in the days of our lives.

Like the farmer, we are to be "patient and stand firm," because Jesus will return to us soon (v. 8). James is implying that God will reward this patience with allowing us to be a part of the fruit of His harvest.

James then explains what our actions would look like if they were to show our patience. We are not to "grumble against" other believers, as we are all working together in the Lord's fields (v. 9). We are not to complain about others, as God will judge us for doing so—and we want to be careful because He will come back soon, so the judgment will be soon also!

James uses another example to complete his argument. He explains that while we are in this world, we can look to the Old Testament prophets for examples of patience and strength (v. 10). Though they suffered greatly, they showed extreme patience as they worked in the Lord's field, waiting for God to reveal His Messiah to the world. **As James notes, all those who persevered by obeying God while waiting for His work to come to fruition are blessed.** Their perseverance was a result of their obedience.

To conclude, James offers Job as an example. When bad things happened to Job, he struggled to trust God. But he remained faithful to the end, and God blessed him as a result (Job

42:7–17). God's blessing on those who persevere reveals that "the Lord is full of compassion and mercy" (James 5:11). As we persevere in our faith, we too can experience the same blessing.

What does showing patience in the face of suffering look like today?

How can our perseverance testify to the goodness of Jesus?

Day 28

Read James 5:12

The last chunk of wisdom James grants to his readers seems short and unexpected. "Above all," he begins, speaking to his fellow "brothers and sisters" as if this is his final point (James 5:12). And it is this: we must not swear—"not by heaven or by earth" nor, as he adds, by any other kind of oath (v. 12). What is this "swearing" of which James speaks?

First, it does not refer to crude or vulgar language. Second, it does not mean commitment, such as we may make to our country as a citizen, at least as long as that commitment does not interfere with our faithfulness to God. Third, it also does not refer to promises, at least when promise is understood to mean an agreement.

James clearly means something much stronger, such as an oath or a contract between two parties that is sealed with statements to strengthen the pact. In this case, if we make an oath with someone else *on heaven's throne* (for example), then we have usurped God's authority to make agreements with people. This kind of oath signals that we believe we are greater than God.

James instructs us to simply say "yes" and "no" when we make agreements with others. As he does throughout his book, he echoes the teaching of Jesus (Matthew 5:37).

This final thought is unexpected, as we might think James would save more important bits of wisdom for last (he does, but not as a warning; see James 5:19–20). Since the beginning, readers of the book of James have wondered why this short proverb is here, and there are many possible reasons.

Here's the one I believe fits best with what we have learned from James: as Jesus's followers, we should be unambiguous about who we are. If we follow Jesus, and if our wisdom for living comes from heaven, then we want to be as clear as possible about that with others. But if we fail to follow Jesus and start deriving our wisdom from the lies that circulate in our world, then we are no longer clear about who we are. We are "like a wave of the sea, blown and tossed by the wind" (1:6). We are "double-minded," unstable in all that we do (1:8).

When we follow the wisdom that comes down from heaven, we will show it in our words and deeds (3:13–16). **If we make oaths, violating God's plan in word and deed, we reveal a true double-mindedness in ourselves.** To James, this may be the ultimate test of character.

What types of swearing do we encounter today? How can we avoid swearing?

Are there situations in life where making "yes" and "no" our way of speaking brings greater glory to God?

Day 29

Read James 5:13–18

As James brings his letter to a close, he turns to two positive actions that believers should exhibit in their lives. The first of these is to pray—to speak to God—to bring about praise, confession, and healing.

James opens with three possibilities (James 5:13–14). If either of these things should happen—being in trouble, being happy, or being sick—prayer is the answer. If we are in trouble, we should go to God with our troubles. If we are happy, we should go to God with thanks. If we are sick, we should call the church together and pray for healing.

Some of us today may find it hard to include prayers for healing with prayers of need or thanksgiving. But James's words suggest that praying for healing is as basic to the faith as praying for help during times of trouble. If we ask God to save us when we are in danger, we should expect Him to do the same when we are sick (v. 15). Similarly, James goes on to say, when we ask God to work in our lives through prayer, part of that should be asking to be forgiven our sins (v. 15). If we ask, God will forgive.

From our modern viewpoint, it might seem strange for James to link physical healing to the forgiveness of sins. Today, these strike us as two very different issues. Modern medicine is built on the idea of discovering physical cures for physical illness, and it does not try to address the role of prayer or forgiveness when it comes to healing. In James's time, however, people assumed they were interrelated. Many believed that sin affected physical health, even to the point of causing sickness (John 9:2).

As believers, we know there is a tighter connection between our soul, our spirit, and our body than modern medicine—as wonderful as it is—can explain. **Therefore, when we get sick, we go to the doctor for physical relief, but we also go to God in prayer for both healing and the forgiveness of sins.** And we go to each other, as brothers and sisters in Christ, to confess our sins so that we may be forgiven, and join in prayer for healing (James 5:16). When we are sick, our expectancy for physical healing is in medicine, but our hope is in the Lord.

James explains this with an example from the life of Elijah (vv. 17–18). Nevertheless, he does not want his readers to idolize or romanticize the prophet; Elijah, he says, was human just like us (v. 17). Elijah prayed earnestly, in faith, and God answered his prayer. Later, Elijah prayed earnestly, in faith, *for the opposite*, and God answered his prayer.

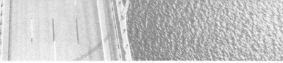

When we pray earnestly and with faith, God moves. Not because He has to but because He wants to. Remember: "The prayer of a righteous person is powerful and effective" (v. 16).

When should we pray? What should we pray for? How can the examples that James gives improve our prayer life?

What does James mean when he talks about a "prayer offered in faith" (James 5:15)? How is that kind of prayer different from other kinds of prayers (for example, prayers for luck or of need, or similar kinds of prayer offered by non believers)?

Day 30

Read James 5:19–20

At first glance, the last words James writes may seem a little flat, ending on a low note. Far from it! These last words are a powerful reminder of the importance of our actions. They serve as a fitting conclusion to James's call to live a life in which our actions are consistent with our beliefs.

James encourages his readers with a scenario (James 5:19). It is hypothetical, but no doubt one that he encountered in his own ministry: What if someone allows himself to be pulled away from the faith? What can be done? James makes it clear that if a brother or sister "should wander from the truth" (v. 19), it is possible for another believer to bring him or her back to the truth.

This raises the question: Why doesn't James just speak directly to the wayward person?

It could be that those wandering are not open to reading his letter (or the Bible). However, James does speak to his readers as if they are themselves capable of falling away ("if one of *you* should wander from the truth", v. 19, emphasis added). The simple fact is that we are all capable of making a wrong turn in life.

Each of us goes through this world facing temptations on every side

especially the temptation to turn away from the truth of the gospel. We don't intend to move away from God, but the world tries to pull us away from the truth, bit by bit. We give in to doubts, we show favoritism, we let our tongues get the better of us, we fail to show our faith in our deeds, we make judgments in the place of God, we acquire wealth to benefit only ourselves, and we make oaths usurping God's role. In short, if we are not careful, we will succumb to a wisdom that springs from the world in which we live.

For those of us who hold on to the kind of wisdom that comes from heaven, James urges us to call those who have given in to the world to come back to living for the Lord. If we do this, we will potentially save their souls from eternal death, and we will bring about the forgiveness of many sins in their lives (v. 20). We will help a person move from being double-minded to being single-minded. Loving a brother or sister back to Jesus is an incredible victory!

This fits in with James's purpose for his letter: to urge us not only to speak as if Christ is risen but also to act as if He is risen. As New Testament scholar Douglas Moo explains, "Not only should the readers of James 'do' the words he has written; they should be deeply concerned to see that others 'do' them also."[3] May we too always "do" the words of the gospel, until Jesus returns! Amen.

[3] Douglas J. Moo, *James: An Introduction and Commentary*, Tyndale New Testament Commentaries 16 (Downers Grove: InterVarsity, 1985), 196.

How can we tell if a brother or sister has wandered from the truth?

In what ways can we "love" a brother or sister back to the truth?

The JourneyThrough® Series
US Editions

Journey through Psalms 1–50, Mike Raiter

Journey through Matthew, Mike Raiter

Journey through Mark, Robert M. Solomon

Journey through Luke, Mike Raiter

Journey through John, David Cook

Journey through Acts, David Cook

Journey through Romans, David Cook

Journey through Colossians and Philemon, Mike Raiter

Journey through James, Douglas Estes

Help us get the word out!

Our Daily Bread Publishing exists to feed the soul with the Word of God.

If you appreciated this book, please let others know.

- Pick up another copy to give as a gift.
- Share a link to the book or mention it on social media.
- Write a review on your blog, on a bookseller's website, or at our own site (odb.org/store).
- Recommend this book for your church, book club, or small group.

Connect with us:

[f] @ourdailybread

[Instagram] @ourdailybread

[Twitter] @ourdailybread

Our Daily Bread Publishing
PO Box 3566
Grand Rapids, Michigan 49501 USA

[✉] books@odb.org